The Porch

A Space For Teaching, Learning, Connecting and Restoration

Elishea H. Barlow

Copyright 2020, The Porch
by Elishea Barlow
ISBN: 978-0-578-72096-8

All rights reserved. No part of this publication may be reproduced, distributed, or transmitted in any form or by any means, including photocopying, recording, or other electronic or mechanical methods, without the prior written permission of the author, except in the case of brief quotations embodied in critical reviews and certain other noncommercial uses permitted by copyright law.

Book cover design and interior layout provided by SelfPublishMe™ Publishing Consulting and Book Design Services for Independent Authors.
www.selfpublishme.com |
email: info@selfpublishme.com

Content

Dedication	5
Introduction	7
Sharing and Solitude	11
Lessons	27
Service	35
Connection	41
Generational	47
Preparation	55
Memories From my Childhood on the Porch	61
A Special Place	71

Dedication

I dedicate this book to those who believe in the acceptance of Jesus Christ as our Lord and Savior. I pray that His peace envelopes you each day and His grace and mercy are always welcomed in your lives. May your spiritual porch, the entrance of your heart, be open always to the sharing of His goodness by the witness of others through the lives you live.

Habakkuk 3:18

"Yet I will rejoice in the Lord, I will joy in the God of my salvation."

Introduction

Porch, according to Websters Merriam Dictionary is: "a covered area adjoining an entrance to a building and usually having a separate roof."

My name is Elishea.

This is not a story, but more of an observation and my version of shared experiences. As you read, I encourage you to think of your own experiences and enjoy your porch.

Take time
to journal
your
experiences
today.

8 THE PORCH

The Porch

Sharing and Solitude

A porch can be
a place of solitude
and for peaceful thinking.
It can be a gathering place
for friends and family.

I remember fun activities of playing and having my hair braided on the porch. Many activities may occur on the porch. Decisions and business deals have been made on the porch.

Wisdom of grandmothers and grandfathers are shared on the porch.

Secrets of sisters are told on the porch. Arguments by brothers are intensely expressed on the porch. Whom have you shared with today?

G entle breezes are felt on the porch. A cup of tea or coffee during an early sunrise meditation is enjoyed on the porch.

Thoughts of the day and releases of stress during an evening sunset can be experienced on the porch.

What have you released today?

Love blossoms with the experience of a first goodnight kiss while relished on the porch.

Memories of loved ones are expressed and shared on the porch.

Who have you thought of today?

THE PORCH **23**

Do you have a porch? What does your porch say about you? Is it cared for?

Is it a part of your family or just your home?

24 THE PORCH

The Porch

Lessons

My grandmother had a porch. It was spacious with many chairs to invite the sitting of others for conversation, food or rest. To her grandchildren, it was a space to play and be close to grandma. Grandma told many stories on her porch. Therefore, lessons of life were told on that porch, sometimes directly or indirectly by listening to the conversations she had with aunts, uncles, parents and other adults.

I used to say, *"There's grandma sitting on the porch."*

What I realize now is that grandma was caring for us and teaching us, when we were on the porch.

My grandma died; however, some of my fondest memories are being with her on the porch. I didn't realize the importance of a porch until recently.

The death of my father opened my eyes to the life of a porch.

My father also had a porch. He too shared much insight of life and living on his porch. A cigarette, a fly swatter and laughter are some memories of my porch-sitting with my dad. A wave to passersby in cars, on bikes and on foot provided a connected force from those of us on the porch to those we saw.

Whom have you connected with recently?

The Porch

Service

The porch is often a place for service: A place to give or to receive that which is given. Many times the letter of a loved one or friend is left by a friendly postal provider in the box on your porch. The bills you pay, the products and services you receive are often collected from the same box on the porch, if you're fortunate to have one on the porch. The request of donations and the pick up of items being donated are presented on the convenience of your porch.

Uncommon friendships are sometimes developed on the porch. The elderly woman who lives alone looks forward to the brief conversation enjoyed from the daily visit of the postal provider. Talks of the weather, the business of their day, the awaited letter from a loved one, bills and the daily happenings or gossip of the neighbors create the conversations enjoyed. The welcoming of the daily meal by the volunteer stranger has grown into an anticipated visit of now, a caring friend because of conversations on the porch.

Do you know someone
who would appreciate a nice meal?

The Porch

Connection

A surprise gift at Christmas from a neighbor may be left in the corner of your porch. Oh how nice! Dinner to a grieving family may be presented with prayer and sympathy from the steps of the porch.

How do you use your porch? Is it empty? Is it hidden? If so, what are you hiding? Does it yearn to be used and shared? Step away. Take a walk around the neighborhood. How many porches say "welcome, love is here." As you walk toward your house, does the sight of your porch say "welcome home?"

The Porch

Generational

Gaps between a generation decrease when conversations of encouragement, ideas, goals and aspirations are shared and heard on the porch.

Our young people whom I call "generation earbuds" may appear at times to not hear you, but please don't be fooled, your words and actions are loud and clear.

Be cautious of your time in still moments. Porch-talk with lessons may soon be lost, or will it? Allow them to see community, communication and support of the human spirit. Are you willing to take the challenge for "generation earbuds." Sometimes, its not all talk. Allow your porch to be a snapshot of the life they see. What does your snapshot convey?

Clean your porch, people see it daily. Be proud of its' presentation. Share it and allow others to share it with you. Enjoy it and allow it to be enjoyed. Teach from it and allow it to be a stage for learning.

Are you willing to be a teacher?
What are you teaching?

The Porch

Preparation

It doesn't matter the size of your porch. What matters are the lessons learned and taught, the giving and receiving of love and respect and the sharing of personal interactions. My mother's porch was small, oh but the memories of preparation for life. The ringing of our doorbell for "trick or treating" always began on our porch. The receipt of our treat always came with lessons of safety prior to our adventure.

Give your children lessons of safety prior to leaving your porch. Leaving the porch is the initiated process of leaving home and entering society.

What are your instructions as they leave?

Do your instructions end with a kiss and a wave from the porch?

A memory of love and security.

The Porch

Memories From my Childhood on the Porch

I remember the safety of my mothers' small porch back in the day when I was young. For a while my siblings and I were considered "latch-key kids". My mother who was an excellent school teacher would at times be at work when we got home from school. Upon her return, we knew we'd better be home and in the house when she got there. I remember one day not having my key. I sat on the porch until she arrived. I felt safe, I read, I did my homework and I talked to friends from across the street. I knew if I weren't in the house, that I'd better be on the porch... and I was.

Can your porch be a place of refuge?
If not, why?
What can be done to make your porch a safe place to retreat?

Some of my happiest and warmest memories of porch activities included getting my hair braided. Every summer when I was a child, with great anticipation, I enjoyed sitting on the porch of my aunts in small town Oklahoma to have my hair braided by one of my cousins. They would put in designs and beads of different colors. I loved it! I sat quietly and listened to various conversations going on by those who were older as they took their time to make me feel beautiful.

Have you uplifted someone lately?

What did you do?

Name a childhood memory of your porch.

As I got older in my teen years, I had a friend who lived nearby who would braid my hair while we had conversations of boys, school, and our future ambitions. We practiced singing and talked of having neighborhood talent shows. Additionally, we fantasied about the money we would make and yes, how we would spend it. Oh how fun!!

Have you involved your neighbor in any of your activities lately?

Do you share inspiration with them?

What are your neighbors' names?

What can you do to be an inspiration to someone?

It really doesn't take a lot. More than you know or imagine: simple kindness from the heart can be all the uplifting and inspiration that someone needs. Try it!

The Porch

A Special Place

Your porch should be a special place. Can Jesus meet you there? Does He speak to you there? Is it a place where you can study His word? Solomons' porch was a place where Jesus was often found as it was at the temple of Jerusalem where many feasts and gatherings occurred (John 10:23). It was a place to congregate as many did when the apostles performed signs and wonders, a place referenced during the healing of the lame man by Peter and John (Acts 3:11, 5:12). Do you feel better on your porch? Is there a "calming" of your spirit, or is it a place like Bethesda where activity or movement was anticipated? Bethesda was a pool surrounded by five porches. Many people waited on the porches in order to receive healing by being the first to enter into the pool when the angel would "move" the water (John 5:2). Do you anticipate a "movement" or "troubling" of the Lords' spirit within you in order to receive His miracles? Do you look for grace and mercy? They're still available. While on the porch at the pool, Jesus asked a man living with a disability if he were willing to accept His will and be made whole; through obedience the man walked from the porch (John: 5: 6). Do you feel complete? He continues to offer his will. Are you willing to accept it?

Know that your porch is a special place. It can be a place of solitude, safety, service, security, wisdom, memories and yes if accepted—Salvation.

www.ingramcontent.com/pod-product-compliance
Lightning Source LLC
Chambersburg PA
CBHW042009150426
43195CB00002B/68